SHOHEI OHTANI

BY ETHAN OLSON

Apex is distributed by North Star Editions:
sales@northstareditions.com | 888-417-0195

Produced for Apex by Red Line Editorial.

Photographs ©: Brandon Sloter/Icon Sportswire/AP Images, cover; Kyodo/AP Images, 1, 6, 8–9, 13, 14–15, 18–19, 26–27; Nick Wosika/Icon Sportswire/AP Images, 4–5, 22–23; Irwin, La Broad, & Pudlin/Library of Congress, 9; Shutterstock Images, 10–11, 16–17; Charlie Riedel/AP Images, 20–21, 29; Jack Dempsey/AP Images, 24–25

Library of Congress Control Number: 2023900130

ISBN
978-1-63738-559-3 (hardcover)
978-1-63738-613-2 (paperback)
978-1-63738-717-7 (ebook pdf)
978-1-63738-667-5 (hosted ebook)

Printed in the United States of America
Mankato, MN
082023

NOTE TO PARENTS AND EDUCATORS

Apex books are designed to build literacy skills in striving readers. Exciting, high-interest content attracts and holds readers' attention. The text is carefully leveled to allow students to achieve success quickly. Additional features, such as bolded glossary words for difficult terms, help build comprehension.

TABLE OF CONTENTS

CHAPTER 1

HUGE HIT 4

CHAPTER 2

LIFE IN JAPAN 10

CHAPTER 3

MOVE TO AMERICA 16

CHAPTER 4

MLB STAR 22

COMPREHENSION QUESTIONS • 28
GLOSSARY • 30
TO LEARN MORE • 31
ABOUT THE AUTHOR • 31
INDEX • 32

HUGE HIT

The Los Angeles Angels face the Oakland A's. It's the fifth **inning**, and the Angels have the lead. Shohei Ohtani steps up to the plate.

Shohei Ohtani is usually third in the batting order.
This spot often goes to a team's best all-around hitter.

The A's pitcher gets ready to throw. Ohtani watches the ball speed toward the plate. He takes a huge swing.

FAST FACT

In 2022, Ohtani hit 34 home runs. That ranked fourth in the American League.

The Los Angeles Angels played the Oakland A's on May 14, 2022.

Ohtani runs around the bases after hitting his 100th home run.

Ohtani's bat makes contact. The ball flies high above center field and over the wall. It's Ohtani's 100th **career** home run.

MAKING HISTORY

Ohtani excels at both hitting and pitching. In 2022, he became the second MLB player to hit at least 100 home runs and strike out at least 250 batters. Only Babe Ruth had done that before.

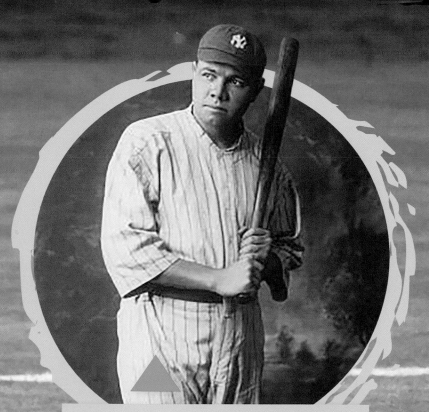

Babe Ruth was one of the greatest baseball players ever. He played in MLB from 1914 to 1935.

CHAPTER 2

LIFE IN JAPAN

Shohei Ohtani grew up in Ōshū, Japan. He had an athletic family. His father played **amateur** baseball. He taught Shohei how to play.

Ōshū is a city in northeastern Japan. This area is known for its beautiful scenery.

From a young age, Shohei showed great talent. Most baseball players focus on either hitting or pitching. But Shohei practiced both.

FAST FACT

During a middle school game, Shohei recorded 17 of the 18 outs with strikeouts.

By high school, Shohei could already throw fastballs over 99 miles per hour (160 km/h).

After high school, Shohei went right to Nippon **Professional** Baseball. That is Japan's top baseball **league**. He became one of its best hitters and pitchers.

AWARD WINNER

Shohei played pro baseball in Japan from 2013 to 2017. During that time, he was named to five **All-Star** teams. He also won an **MVP** award in 2016.

As a pro player in Japan, Shohei played for the Hokkaido Nippon-Ham Fighters.

CHAPTER 3

MOVE TO AMERICA

In 2017, Ohtani decided to leave Japan and join MLB. Many teams wanted him to play for them. He chose the Los Angeles Angels.

The Los Angeles Angels play at Angel Stadium in Anaheim, California.

Ohtani pitched in 10 games for the Angels during the 2018 season.

Ohtani quickly became an MLB star. Fans were impressed by his speedy pitches and huge hits. He won Rookie of the Year after his first season.

FAST FACT

Fans gave Ohtani a nickname. They called him "Sho-time."

SHORT SEASON

Because of COVID-19, each MLB team had only 60 games instead of 162 in 2020. Ohtani played 46 games that season. He had 29 hits and 7 home runs.

Ohtani struggled the next two seasons. He had **surgery** on his elbow. He took a break from pitching for the 2019 season. And he pitched just twice in 2020.

Ohtani had 153 at bats during the 2020 season.

CHAPTER 4

MLB STAR

In 2021, Ohtani made a huge comeback. He hit 46 home runs that season. He was also one of baseball's best pitchers. He was voted American League MVP.

Ohtani hits a home run against the Minnesota Twins.

Ohtani did not let any batters on base during the first inning of the 2021 All-Star Game.

The Angels struggled in 2021. They won less than half their games. But Ohtani made the All-Star team.

TWO-WAY ALL-STAR

Ohtani was the starting pitcher and **leadoff hitter** in the 2021 All-Star Game. He was the first player to make the team as both a hitter and a pitcher.

Players like Ohtani who hit and pitch are called two-way players.

The Angels had another tough year in 2022. But Ohtani kept setting records. Fans were excited to keep watching him.

FAST FACT

In 2022, Ohtani became the first MLB player to finish a season with at least 30 home runs and 10 wins as a pitcher.

COMPREHENSION QUESTIONS

Write your answers on a separate piece of paper.

1. Write a few sentences describing the main ideas of Chapter 2.

2. If you played baseball, would you rather hit or pitch? Why?

3. When did Ohtani stop playing in Japan?
    - **A.** 2013
    - **B.** 2017
    - **C.** 2021

4. Why would most baseball players focus on either hitting or pitching?
    - **A.** because the two jobs happen at different times
    - **B.** because the two jobs require different skills
    - **C.** because doing both is not possible

5. What does **athletic** mean in this book?

*He had an **athletic** family. His father played amateur baseball.*

    A. good at sports

    B. having many people

    C. talking quietly

6. What does **impressed** mean in this book?

*Ohtani quickly became an MLB star. Fans were **impressed** by his speedy pitches and huge hits.*

    A. bored and angry

    B. shocked and scared

    C. pleased and surprised

Answer key on page 32.

GLOSSARY

All-Star
Having to do with the best players in a league.

amateur
Someone who doesn't get paid to play a sport.

career
The full amount of time a player spends in a sport or league.

inning
Part of a baseball game. A regular baseball game has nine innings. More innings are added if the game is tied.

leadoff hitter
The batter who goes first in the lineup.

league
A group of teams that play one another.

MVP
An award given to the best player in a sport or league.

professional
Having to do with people who get paid for what they do.

surgery
When doctors make cuts in the body to solve problems.

TO LEARN MORE

BOOKS

Donnelly, Patrick. *Los Angeles Angels*. Minneapolis: Abdo
Publishing, 2023.

Hewson, Anthony K. *Baseball Records*. Lake Elmo, MN:
Focus Readers, 2021.

Walker, Hubert. *The World Series*. Mendota Heights, MN:
Apex Editions, 2023.

ONLINE RESOURCES

Visit **www.apexeditions.com** to find links and resources
related to this title.

ABOUT THE AUTHOR

Ethan Olson is a sportswriter based in Minneapolis,
Minnesota. He is dedicated to sports but also enjoys making
music and exploring nature in his free time. He'd love to cover
a World Cup one day.

INDEX

A
All-Star, 15, 24–25
American League, 22

C
COVID-19, 20

J
Japan, 10, 14, 15, 16

L
Los Angeles Angels, 4, 16, 24, 27

M
MVP, 15, 22

N
Nippon Professional Baseball, 14

O
Oakland A's, 4, 7
Ōshū, Japan, 10

P
pitcher, 7, 12, 14, 18, 21, 25, 27

R
Ruth, Babe, 9

ANSWER KEY:
1. Answers will vary; 2. Answers will vary; 3. B; 4. B; 5. A; 6. C

AMERICAN ALLIGATOR VS. WILD BOAR

BY NATHAN SOMMER

BELLWETHER MEDIA • MINNEAPOLIS, MN

Torque brims with excitement
perfect for thrill-seekers of all kinds.
Discover daring survival skills, explore
uncharted worlds, and marvel at mighty
engines and extreme sports. In *Torque* books,
anything can happen. Are you ready?

This edition first published in 2023 by Bellwether Media, Inc.

No part of this publication may be reproduced in whole or in part without written
permission of the publisher. For information regarding permission, write to
Bellwether Media, Inc., Attention: Permissions Department,
6012 Blue Circle Drive, Minnetonka, MN 55343.

Library of Congress Cataloging-in-Publication Data

Names: Sommer, Nathan, author.
Title: American alligator vs. wild boar / by Nathan Sommer.
Other titles: American alligator versus wild boar
Description: Minneapolis, MN : Bellwether Media, Inc., 2023. | Series:
    Torque. Animal battles | Includes bibliographical references and index.
    | Audience: Ages 7-12 | Audience: Grades 4-6 | Summary: "Amazing
    photography accompanies engaging information about the fighting
    advantages of American alligators and wild boars. The combination of
    high-interest subject matter and light text is intended for students in
    grades 3 through 7"– Provided by publisher.
Identifiers: LCCN 2022038241 (print) | LCCN 2022038242 (ebook) | ISBN
    9798886871647 (library binding) | ISBN 9798886872125 (paperback) | ISBN
    9798886872903 (ebook)
Subjects: LCSH: American alligator–Juvenile literature. | Wild
    boar–Juvenile literature.
Classification: LCC QL666.C925 S635 2023 (print) | LCC QL666.C925 (ebook)
    | DDC 597.98/4–dc23/eng/20220829
LC record available at https://lccn.loc.gov/2022038241
LC ebook record available at https://lccn.loc.gov/2022038242

Text copyright © 2023 by Bellwether Media, Inc. TORQUE and associated logos are
trademarks and/or registered trademarks of Bellwether Media, Inc.

Editor: Kieran Downs   Designer: Josh Brink

Printed in the United States of America, North Mankato, MN.

TABLE OF CONTENTS

THE COMPETITORS 4

SECRET WEAPONS 10

ATTACK MOVES 16

READY, FIGHT! 20

GLOSSARY 22

TO LEARN MORE 23

INDEX 24

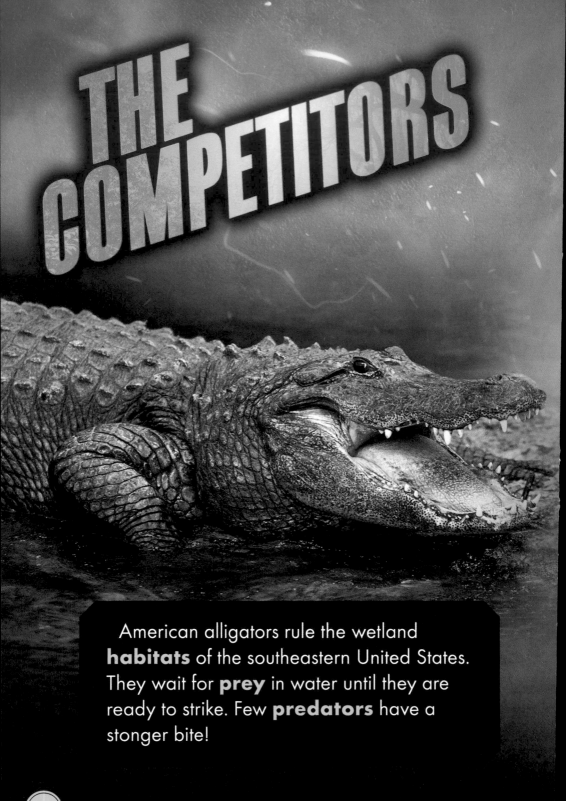

THE COMPETITORS

American alligators rule the wetland **habitats** of the southeastern United States. They wait for **prey** in water until they are ready to strike. Few **predators** have a stonger bite!

But some prey put up a fight against the hungry alligators. Wild boars team up to take on strong challengers. What happens when alligators and boars come face-to-face?

AMERICAN ALLIGATOR PROFILE

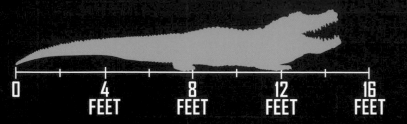

0	4 FEET	8 FEET	12 FEET	16 FEET

LENGTH
**UP TO 15 FEET
(4.6 METERS)**

WEIGHT
**UP TO 1,000 POUNDS
(454 KILOGRAMS)**

HABITAT

RIVERS LAKES MARSHES SWAMPS

AMERICAN ALLIGATOR RANGE

RANGE

American alligators have existed for around 150 million years! They are the largest **reptiles** in North America. They grow up to 15 feet (4.6 meters) long. They weigh up to 1,000 pounds (454 kilograms).

These beasts are **apex predators**. They live in freshwater wetlands. Most prefer slow-moving rivers.

Wild boars are the largest wild pigs. They have stocky bodies, large heads, and sharp **tusks**. These pigs roam grasslands and woodlands around the world. They prefer thick forests near bodies of water.

Male wild boars are mostly **solitary**. Females live and hunt in groups of up to 100. These groups are called sounders.

TUSK

WILD BOAR PROFILE

36 INCHES

24 INCHES

12 INCHES

0

HEIGHT
UP TO 35.4 INCHES
(90 CENTIMETERS)
AT THE SHOULDER

WEIGHT
UP TO 600 POUNDS
(272 KILOGRAMS)

HABITAT

WOODLANDS

GRASSLANDS

SWAMPS

WILD BOAR RANGE

RANGE

SECRET WEAPONS

SPEED IN BURSTS

American alligators are fast on land, too. They run in short bursts at speeds of around 30 miles (48 kilometers) per hour!

STRONG TAIL

American alligators use their strong tails to swim fast. They reach speeds of 20 miles (32 kilometers) per hour in water. This allows them to easily catch most prey.

30 MILES (48 KILOMETERS) PER HOUR

WILD BOAR

28 MILES (45 KILOMETERS) PER HOUR

HUMAN

Wild boars are also fast. They run at speeds of up to 30 miles (48 kilometers) per hour. They use this speed to charge at enemies.

American alligators have incredibly powerful jaws. They pair these with strong teeth to capture prey and hold it in place. One bite can crack bones and turtle's shells!

ALLIGATOR TOOTH SIZE

3 INCHES —

2.5 INCHES
(6.4 CENTIMETERS)

2 INCHES —

1 INCH —

0 —

A LOT OF TEETH

Alligator teeth grow back when they are damaged or broken. Some alligators go through 3,000 teeth in their lifetime!

Wild boars have long, razor-sharp
canine teeth called tusks. They use these
to cut enemies. Tusks can grow up to
19 inches (48 centimeters) long in males!

STRONG TAILS

**POWERFUL
JAWS**

**THICK, SCALY
SKIN**

SCALY SKIN

American alligators have thick, scaly skin on their backs. This protects them against bites and cuts from enemies. It also helps them easily **camouflage** in water.

SECRET WEAPONS

WILD BOAR

SPEED

SHARP TUSKS

LARGE GROUPS

Female wild boars fight in groups. They use growls to **communicate** with their groups and warn them of danger. Together they can scare off much larger animals.

ATTACK MOVES

American alligators **stalk** and **ambush** prey. They blend in with the dark waters of their homes. They quietly swim up to prey until they are close enough to attack.

Wild boars fight when threatened. They charge at enemies to trip them. Then they attack once the enemies are on the ground!

SWIMMING PIGS

Wild boars are strong swimmers. They can swim for miles at a time without resting.

Prey rarely escapes the strong jaws of American alligators. Small prey is often swallowed whole. Larger animals are dragged underwater and drowned.

Wild boars have a great sense of smell. They can smell things more than 5 miles (8 kilometers) away!

Wild boars use teamwork to their **advantage**. They run into enemies as a group. They use their tusks to attack the bodies of enemies. The large group can take on most attackers.

READY, FIGHT!

An American alligator creeps up on a wild boar. It is about to attack! The boar hears the alligator step on a leaf. It lets out a growl to warn its group.

The boars charge at the alligator. The reptile runs away from the group. The wild boars have outnumbered the apex predator today!

GLOSSARY

advantage—something that an animal has or can do better than other animals

ambush—to carry out a surprise attack

apex predators—animals at the top of the food chain that are not preyed upon by other animals

camouflage—to use colors and patterns to help an animal hide in its surroundings

canine teeth—long, pointed teeth that are often the sharpest in the mouth

communicate—to share thoughts and feelings using sounds, faces, and actions

habitats—the homes or areas where animals prefer to live

predators—animals that hunt other animals for food

prey—animals that are hunted by other animals for food

reptiles—cold-blooded animals that have backbones and lay eggs

solitary—related to living alone

stalk—to follow closely and quietly

tusks—long, pointed teeth that are visible outside of an animal's mouth

TO LEARN MORE

AT THE LIBRARY

Downs, Kieran. *Nile Crocodile vs. Hippopotamus.* Minneapolis, Minn.: Bellwether Media, 2022.

O'Brien, Cynthia. *Bringing Back the American Alligator.* New York, N.Y.: Crabtree Publishing, 2019.

Reynolds, Donna. *Wild Boars in the Forest.* New York, N.Y.: Gareth Stevens Publishing, 2023.

ON THE WEB

FACTSURFER

Factsurfer.com gives you a safe, fun way to find more information.

1. Go to www.factsurfer.com

2. Enter "American alligator vs. wild boar" into the search box and click Q.

3. Select your book cover to see a list of related content.

INDEX

ambush, 16
apex predators, 7, 21
attack, 16, 17, 19, 20
bite, 4, 12, 14
camouflage, 14
charge, 11, 17, 21
females, 8, 15
groups, 8, 15, 19, 20, 21
growls, 15, 20
habitats, 4, 6, 7, 8, 9
hunt, 8
jaws, 12, 18
males, 8, 13
North America, 7
predators, 4
prey, 4, 5, 10, 12, 16, 18
range, 4, 6, 9
reptiles, 7, 21

size, 6, 7, 8, 9, 12, 13
skin, 14
smell, 19
solitary, 8
sounders, 8
speed, 10, 11
stalk, 16
swim, 10, 16, 17
tails, 10
teeth, 12, 13
tusks, 8, 13, 19
United States, 4
water, 4, 7, 8, 10, 14, 16, 18
weapons, 14, 15
wild pigs, 8

The images in this book are reproduced through the courtesy of: Deborah Ferrin, cover (alligator); Roberto La Rosa, cover (alligator body); Life On White/ Getty Images, cover (boar); Jeffrey B. Banke, cover (boar eye); WildMedia, pp. 2-3 (boar left), 5 (boar herd), 20, 22-24 (boar left); Martin Prochazkacz, pp. 2-3, 20, 22-24 (boar right); Budimir Jevtic, pp. 2-3, 21, 22-24 (wild boars background); gerard lacz/ Alamy Stock Photo, p. 4; Miroslav Hlavko, p. 5 (wild boar front); scott biales/ Alamy Stock Photo, pp. 6-7; Panther Media/ Alamy Stock Photo, pp. 8-9; Tim Graham/ Getty Images, p. 10; Tierfotoagentur/ m.blue-shado/ Alamy Stock Photo, p. 11; Ed Reschke/ Getty Images, p. 12; Neil_Burton/ Getty Images, p. 13; Andrew Jeffries, p. 14 (strong tails); Steve Byland, p. 14 (powerful jaws); Brittany Mason, p. 14 (thick, scaly skin); Cecile Marion/ Alamy Stock Photo, p. 14 (alligator); Robert Adame, p. 15 (speed); Katerina Iacovides, p. 15 (sharp tusks); MMCez, p. 15 (large groups); Wachira Waharapathom, p. 15 (boars); Daniel Rose, p. 16; Henry Ausloos/ Alamy Stock Photo, p. 17; blickwinkel/Woike/ Alamy Stock Photo, p. 18; WireStock/ Alamy Stock Photo, p. 19; slowmotiongli, p. 21 (alligator).

ANIMAL BATTLES

AMERICAN ALLIGATOR VS. WILD BOAR

ANACONDA VS. JAGUAR

ASIATIC LION VS. BENGAL TIGER

BADGER VS. BOBCAT

BARRACUDA VS. MORAY EEL

DINGO VS. KANGAROO

DUNG BEETLE VS. TARANTULA HAWK

GIANT OTTER VS. CAIMAN

GOLDEN EAGLE VS. GREAT HORNED OWL

GORILLA VS. LEOPARD

GREAT WHITE SHARK VS. KILLER WHALE

GRIZZLY BEAR VS. WOLF PACK

KING COBRA VS. MONGOOSE

LION VS. CAPE BUFFALO

LION VS. HYENA CLAN

MANTIS SHRIMP VS. LIONFISH

MOUNTAIN LION VS. COYOTE

NILE CROCODILE VS. HIPPOPOTAMUS

OSTRICH VS. CHEETAH

POLAR BEAR VS. WALRUS

PRAYING MANTIS VS. BLACK WIDOW SPIDER

SCORPION VS. TARANTULA

SKUNK VS. RACCOON

SNOW LEOPARD VS. WILD YAK

TIGER SHARK VS. LEOPARD SEAL

WOLVERINE VS. HONEY BADGER

ISBN 979-8-88687-212-5

9 798886 872125

BELLWETHER
www.bellwethermedia.com

OSTRICH VS. CHEETAH